*" The first requisite to happiness
is that a man be born in a
famous city."*

PLUTARCH.

With an Artist in Winchester

Written and illustrated
by
J.L.Northeast, ATD

LAURENCE OXLEY
Broad Street, Alresford, Hampshire

ISBN 0 9504096 0 X

Printed and bound in Great Britain by
The Scolar Press Limited, Ilkley, Yorkshire

FOREWORD

It gives me great pleasure, as Mayor of the new City of Winchester, to write a short foreword to this reprinted edition of the late Mr. J. L. Northeast's book "With an Artist in Winchester" which was first published in 1961. I was particularly glad, too, since it was as Mayor of the "old" city that I wrote the foreword for the book's second edition in 1967.

Much has happened to Winchester since 1961. Some of its most important buildings, so well illustrated in the book, have been the subject of repair and restoration, amongst them the Chesil Rectory, 40–41 High Street, part of God-Begot, and St. Swithun's Church and gate. An important section of the High Street has become a foot-way from which vehicular traffic is barred. There has also been much demolition and new building. The domestic scale of Winchester is vanishing in the 1970's, and it is no small part of the value of this particular book that it depicts Winchester's historic buildings against the background of the old domestic architecture. I wish this new publication every success.

BARBARA CARPENTER TURNER

19 March, 1975

The Mayor's Parlour,
Guildhall,
Winchester.

To
My Mother,
Eileen and Coral.

1967.

CONTENTS

1. The Westgate
2. The High Street
3. The Oldest Bar in England
4. The Godbegot
5. The Godbegot—North Side
6. The Buttercross
7. The Market Square
8. The Eclipse Inn
9. The Cathedral in Spring
10. The Cathedral—North Transept
11. The Cathedral—South Transept
12. Early Norman Arcading and the Deanery
13. The Pilgrims' Hall
14. Cheyney Court
15. The Prior's Gate
16. The Kingsgate
17. Ruins of Wolvesey Castle
18. College Gateway
19. The Trusty Servant
20. War Memorial Cloisters—College
21. The Church of St. Cross
22. Beaufort Hall, St. Cross
23. St. Cross from the Archway
24. In the Church of St. Cross
25. St. Cross from the Lily Pond
26. Ancient Houses, St. Cross
27. The City Mill
28. St. John's Croft and the Blue Boar Inn
29. Chesil Rectory
30. St. John's Hospital
31. Abbey House
32. King Alfred's Statue

1. THE WESTGATE

" It is no small thing to live in a city of memories
Where, not here and there, but at every turn
The past is brought before us."

ANON.

The outer face of the Westgate once had a bold embattled parapet, which surmounted the heavy overhanging machicolations which are still to be seen and must have given to the gate a much more forbidding but better balanced appearance than it has today. Despite this short-coming, the Westgate is a grand old monument to the days when Winchester was a walled city. Some years ago it was proposed to restore this parapet and had this been done, our gate would have looked more like the Bargate in Southampton.

Today the Westgate is the result of many repairs over hundreds of years but it is generally agreed that the central arch is thirteenth century and was erected during the reign of King Henry III.

Quite apart from the exceptional interest of the small museum in the room over the gate, it is well worth mounting the massive twisting stone stairway and going on to the flat roof to gaze over the City.

The West Gate, Winchester.
13th Century.

J. Ludlow Northea

2. THE HIGH STREET

" With quiet calm the ancient buildings gaze
On a jostling modern world."

ANON.

It is said that Winchester High Street has a greater wealth of historical associations than any other street in England. Certainly for more than three hundred years it was the main street of the capital of England and has much to interest the artist and the sightseer.

In this city many Kings and Queens were crowned and lived and more monarchs lie buried in the Cathedral than in Westminster Abbey. It was here that the Witans, or ancient parliaments met; here were the Royal Treasury and the Royal Mint and here were written the Anglo Saxon Chronicle and the Domesday Book.

Off the High Street is situated Staple Gardens, once the centre of the wool market, hence its name ' Staple '. Here, too, is Trafalgar Street, the spear makers' quarter. Southgate Street marks the old ' Goldstreet ' which was the jewellers' locality. Branching off the High Street are Jewry Street, which was the Jewish quarter (without the City walls) and Parchment Street and Brook Street, which were the sites of the binderies of Winchester, a city famous for its many beautiful manuscripts.

Between the massive Westgate at the top and the splendid statue of King Alfred at the bottom, are many things of interest to see and to sketch. Among these, all within a mile, are the old Guildhall tower, from which the curfew is still rung every evening; the great City Clock of Queen Anne's time and her statue in the niche below, shown in my drawing; the Manor of Godbegot with its untouched Elizabethan timberwork; the Royal Oak with its subterranean bar; the beautiful Butter Cross comfortably set in its attractive corner and the medieval houses of the Pentice.

—HIGH STREET, WINCHESTER—

3. THE OLDEST BAR IN ENGLAND

" As ancient is this hostelry
As any in the land may be."

LONGFELLOW.

The Royal Oak Inn was built in 1630 but beneath it is its most interesting feature, the subterranean Bar known, as the sign board in the High Street tells us, as the ' Oldest Bar in England '. Such a claim is difficult to prove and is advanced also by ' The Trip to Jerusalem ' at Nottingham and several other inns.

Today one enters the Bar by stone steps from the inn above but in the south wall made of rough flint, one can see the top part of a narrow archway well below present ground level, which was the original entrance. This archway is thought by archaeologists to be Saxon work, which would give substance to the claim to be the Oldest Bar in England.

My illustration is drawn from the west end of the Bar and shows the tiny windows in the east wall which are at ground level and admit very little daylight and so the Bar is always artificially lighted. On the left of the drawing is a long, smooth, very worn shove-penny table said to be the oldest in the land, which has been in use for two to three hundred years. The Saxon arch cannot be seen in the drawing but is on the right, opposite the flight of steps.

The ' Oldest Bar ' is a pleasant and interesting place in which to drink and browse in the heat of a summer day, as the Bar is always cool.

"The Oldest Bar in England"
The Royal Oak, Winchester.

4. THE GODBEGOT

" Whoe'er has travelled life's dull round,
Where'er his stages may have been,
May sigh to think he still hath found
The warmest welcome at an inn.

SHENSTONE.

Described in Aethelred's charter as ' The Manor of Godbegot ' it originally extended from St. Peter's Street to the High Street as far as the site of the George Hotel, demolished in 1957.

This ' parcel of land ' was included in King Aethelred's wedding present to Queen Emma. (The Queen is remembered by a room named after her in the hotel and her remains rest in a sarcophagus in the Cathedral Choir.) On her death she left the site to the Priory of St. Swithun in whose hands it remained for eight hundred years. During this period it was independent of civic jurisdiction and was ' a place of sanctuary ' to which criminals fled. In 1866 the Ecclesiastical Commissioners sold it to a private person and, at that time, title deeds of ownership went back for eight hundred years. With the exception of the front façade, the present building is mostly of the sixteenth century, having been built in 1558, to a rectangular plan with a smaller inner court around a well. In 1896 it became the property of a Miss Pamplin, who converted the western portion into an hotel and revived its old, almost forgotten name. In 1908 the admirable restoration of the front, shown in the drawing, was carried out by her. The four dates on the signboard over the side door mark the chief milestones in the history of Godbegot.

"The Godbegot"
Winchester.

J.L. NORTHEAST.

5. THE GODBEGOT—NORTH SIDE

*" I love everything that's old: old friends, old
times, old manners, old books, old wine."*

GOLDSMITH.

In 1957, we had for the first time, an excellent view of the north side of the Manor of Godbegot, after the demolition of buildings used as an ironworks. This revealed the mighty timber frame and mellow brickwork of the genuine sixteenth-century Tudor mansion extending from St. Peter's Street to the Royal Oak Passage. St. Peter's Street was originally known as Fleshmongers' Street because it was the butchers' quarter, but took its present name from the very small church which once stood upon the site of the demolished iron works. The plan of the church is now marked by red brick lines.

The name ' Godbegot ' is of doubtful origin and might have meant ' acquired for God ', or it might be a corruption of " Goodbegot ', and so mean prosaically the ' house of the Goods getter '.

St. George's Street, from which my drawing was made, once led to St. George's Church, which stood at the eastern end of Silver Hill.

GODBEGOT HOTEL (North side)

B

6. THE BUTTER CROSS

" The eye satisfied, embraced the structure,
Never surprised and always enchanted."

ANON.

The Butter Cross is said to be a gift to the City from Cardinal Beaufort, Bishop of Winchester from 1404 to 1447; but, in fact, the 'High Cross', as it was called originally, was in existence by the middle of the fourteenth century.

Many consider the Butter Cross to be the most beautiful city cross in England. Before its restoration it was painted by J. W. M. Turner during his early topographical days, towards the end of the eighteenth century. The restoration was admirably carried out by Sir Gilbert Scott, from an old engraving in 1865. Today it is very much as he left it.

In my drawing, done from the west side, we see King Alfred in his niche. On his left is a timber-framed house, probably of the fourteenth century, and on his right is the beginning of the Pentice, or covered shopping way, where a number of ancient beams have been uncovered within the last year. The timbered house is marred by the incongruous Gothic style window on the second floor, and the house certainly looked better proportioned in an early nineteenth century engraving where it had a heavy carved barge-board.

Roughly marking the central point of the City, the Butter Cross and its corner is dear to the people of Winchester and much used as a meeting place. Its steps, alas, are no longer employed for the sale of butter and eggs, as was once the case, and only the newsvendor sells his papers there now.

Butter Cross Corner, High Street, Winchester.

7. THE MARKET SQUARE

" Where at each coign of every antique street
A memory hath taken root in stone."

LIONEL JOHNSON.

A mixed huddle of pleasant buildings forms a sheltered little area, gay with flowers, in the centre of the City and makes up one of the most charming and characteristic views of Winchester. I call it ' characteristic ' because this little corner contains relics of history from the Conqueror's day to our own, in no dead ' museum ' sense, for this is the very heart of Winchester, warm, pulsating with shoppers, visitors, trade and traffic.

Beneath the arch is a stone pilaster which is a small remnant of William's great palace. Further remains of it are the vast cellars of early Norman date beneath some of the shops facing the Square.

Adjoining the arch is a tall house over a shop front which, at first glance, appears to be of red brick but in fact it is not. It is dressed with thin red tiles laid flat and lined with mortar in an effort to make an old façade look ' modern ', similar to the fashionable red brick houses of 18th century London. So fickle is architectural fashion, however, that within a stone's throw we can see, by walking through Minster Street Passage nearby, the back of a shop which has recently had its ' modern ' stucco removed to reveal its ancient timber and plaster and so restoring its old-fashioned look.

In the centre of my drawing is the grey stone tower which is all that is to be seen of St. Lawrence Church.

Across the blind street was Chalkley's shop, which until recently was distinguished by its old fish sign, a relic of the days when this form of peasant art made business premises known to the illiterate. Gilbert's book shop in the corner has a badge indicating membership of the ' County ' Fire Insurance Company. This was necessary when assistance, in case of fire, came only to those who displayed their ' policy ' in this way.

CHALK
THE SQUARE
Sports CHALK

— THE SQUARE, WINCHESTER. —

8. THE ECLIPSE INN

" Along the varying road of life
In calm content, in toil or strife,
At morn or noon, by night or day,
As time conducts him on his way,
How oft doth man, by care oppressed,
Find in an inn, a place of rest."

W. COOMBE.

The Eclipse Inn, in common with many other buildings now put to a commercial use, was once a rectory, belonging to the Church of St. Lawrence, which stands hidden behind it. There is a pleasant story of how the inn obtained its name. Across the way from it, when it became an inn, was a rival hostelry, the Sun Inn. It was the ambition of the new innkeeper to steal the trade of the Sun. This he ultimately did and ' eclipsed ' him.

History gives us another and far less pleasant incident from the inn's long life. In the seventeenth century Dame Alice Lisle, whose husband had been executed for regicide, gave hospitality to two men of Monmouth's rebellion. She was arrested and stood trial before Judge Jeffreys' ' Bloody Assizes ' at Winchester, where she was sentenced to be drawn on a hurdle and burned alive. The Bishop of Winchester, however, went to the Judge's Lodgings and intervened. Nevertheless, she had to die and on September 2nd, 1685, aged and ill, she stepped from an upper window of the Eclipse and walked over the staging to the raised block and was beheaded. Today the memory of this is kept alive by the tablet on the wall, whilst the Eclipse is a happy, peaceful little inn nestling comfortably between its bigger and younger neighbours.

With its high-pitched roof, heavy decorative barge-board and the bold pattern of its fine oak frame filled with brick and plaster, it is a splendid subject for the pen of the artist and for the camera of the holiday maker. It should be mentioned that the front is actually good modern restoration.

· THE ECLIPSE INN , WINCHESTER. 16ᵀᴴ CENTURY -

9. THE CATHEDRAL IN SPRING

" How reverend is the face of this tall pile
Whose ancient pillars rear their carven heads
To bear aloft its arched and ponderous roof,
By its own weight made steadfast and immovable."

EMERSON.

The best time to see the grey-green length of this vast nave—the longest in Europe—is when the avenue of limes is lightly foliaged with splashes of translucent green and the nuthatch repeats his single clear note in their tops. Great as its length is, the Cathedral was once even longer, as is shown by the foundations of Norman walls extending underground, forty feet further westward.

The west front is the work of Bishop Edington and William of Wykeham. It was Wykeham who demolished the original Norman work, which was in all probability far more beautiful than the plain grid-like façade which he built in the 'new' Perpendicular style of the fifteenth century. The huge west window does little to help the external proportions of the west end of the Cathedral; but to see this window from the inside, when the long, low shafts of a westering sun light the cavernous interior with a warm golden light, is an experience to be remembered.

WINCHESTER CATHEDRAL IN SPRING

10. THE CATHEDRAL—NORTH TRANSEPT

" When we build, let us think we build for ever."

J. RUSKIN.

Salisbury Cathedral, because it is all in one style, is often known as
" the Architects' Cathedral." For contrary reasons, ' Winchester '
might well be described as " the students' cathedral," for within a few
acres one can see examples of church architecture and decoration
which range from the Early Norman style to Late Gothic. The north
transept still shows rugged massive Norman work with characteristic
round arches, simple billet decoration, cushion capitals, plain pilasters
and chamfer bases, built by Bishop Walkelin. It also shows us later
windows fitting uncomfortably under Norman arches, and some
windows which have been completely transformed to the Perpendicular
Gothic. To this style belongs the rose window which today can be
seen from the outside only, since a wooden ceiling in Tudor style was
erected in 1818. This transept escaped with little damage when the
tower fell in 1107. Fortunately it also escaped complete transforma-
tion at the hands of the renovators in the fourteenth and fifteenth
centuries, which, had it taken place, would have given it more unity
but less interest.

The gable end appears incomplete, as in fact it is, for the unfinished
turret on the north-east corner and other features, suggest that it was
intended to flank the gable with two towers.

It is a pity that aggressive iron railings prevent those interested
from wandering close under these ancient walls. During the last few
years extensive ' diggings ' have taken place and it is hoped to add
considerably to the store of knowledge about the Cathedral.

The North Transept
Winchester Cathedral

11. THE CATHEDRAL—south transept

" Hallowed ground before the Normans built."

ANON.

I think this view of the Cathedral from the south-west, together with that from the Dean's garden on the south-east, are the most attractive. The solid pile of the buildings and the old trees shadowing the smooth lawns, combine to harmonise and make a mellow, unspoiled picture.

To an architect this aspect must be particularly interesting for it shows in the south transept both early and late Norman work; and some transitional blind arcading in the pediment. The tower was built in 1107 to replace the earlier one of Bishop Walkelin after its collapse. The opening arcading of the Chapter House is early Norman work, while the Gothic windows of the nave and flying buttresses belong to the Perpendicular style.

Beneath the ancient sundial on the south-west corner is the entrance to the Slype or covered passage way, leading to the east end, and above it can be seen in my drawing the Cathedral library, which is well worth a visit for it houses many rare and beautiful illuminated manuscripts.

—NORMAN ARCADING—
— SOUTH TRANSEPT, WINCHESTER —

12. EARLY NORMAN ARCADING AND THE DEANERY

" With massive arches broad and round
Built ere the art was known,
By pointed aisles and shafted stalk
The arcades of an alleyed walk
To emulate in stone."

SIR WALTER SCOTT.

These fine monolith pillars with their cushion capitals and small round arches, are beautiful examples of early Norman architecture and are remains of the entrance to the early Chapter House. If you look through these arches to your left, you will see the arcading of the monks' seats and across the lawn, the house which was once the home of Mrs. Sumner, founder of the Mothers' Union movement. The large archway in the left foreground leads into the Slype, which gives access to the south transept and then to the bottom of the City.

In the extreme background of my illustration is a house where the Assize Judges live during the time when the court is in session. This building is known as the Judges' lodgings. I recommend you to walk towards it and then turn about, when you will find yourself facing a grand group of buildings—the Deanery, the Restoration Gallery, now used as the Dean's library, and filling the whole background is the South Transept of the Cathedral with its massive Norman tower.

The most noticeable and beautiful feature of the Deanery is the porch with its fine 13th century arches. To the left of these arches is the 15th century Hall which has a magnificent oak roof resting on corbel heads. The building to the right is the 17th century Gallery built by Richard Frampton of Kingsgate Street, with its warm red walls acting as a perfect foil to the green trees and grey stone of the Cathedral. This view of the south transept shows examples of large Norman windows with 14th century mullions built into them. Above these may be seen round Norman arcading interlaced to form pointed arches. This is thought by some authorities to be the origin of the pointed arch and so known as ' transitional '.

Early Norman Arcading & The Deanery,
Cathedral Close, Winchester

13. THE PILGRIMS' HALL

" The Lord is only my support,
And he that doth me feed;
How can I then want anything
Whereof I stand in need."

JOHN BUNYAN.

My drawing shows the interesting open stairway and gallery at the northern end of Pilgrims' Hall, which is to be found in the Cathedral Close near to the Prior's Gate. From the Middle Ages until the early 16th century, the Cathedral church in Winchester was part of St. Swithun's Priory, which was a Benedictine foundation. This monastery and the Shrine of Saint Swithun of Winchester in the Cathedral attracted many pilgrims from this country and the Continent. It was expected of the Order of the Benedictines that its monks should show hospitality to visitors to the monastery and it is obvious that some considerable building must have been set apart for such a purpose.

The monastry and its domestic buildings lay to the south-west of the cathedral and included the building, part of which is shown in my illustration. Although there is no absolute documentary proof as to its original use, the building has been known as ' the Pilgrims' Hall ' since Bishop John Milner, a local historian, suggested in his " History of Winchester " that this was the hall used to house the pilgrims.

The buttresses, the lancet-shaped inner arches of two of the original windows, the carved heads on the ends of the hammer beams and other architectural details are internal evidence that the building probably dates from the early 14th century. The hammer-beam roof trusses, which are part of the original structure, are particularly fine and massive. Some still have the remains of carved heads as terminals and one of these is thought to represent the boy King Edward III after his accession in 1327.

The very fine restoration of this building was completed in 1960.

THE GALLERY, PILGRIMS' HALL, WINCHESTER.

C I

14. CHEYNEY COURT

" Where, on all hands, wondrous with ancient grace,
Grace touch'd with age, rise works of goodliest men."

LIONEL JOHNSON.

With our backs turned to the Deanery and its beautiful thirteenth-century arches, we face one of the finest gems of timber-framed domestic architecture in the country. It seems, from an artist's point of view, that this corner could not be improved.

Cheyney Court looks at its best when the venerable wistaria hangs its pale mauve flowers over the Prior's Gate and much of the timbered houses. Prior's Gate, seen in the drawing, leads almost directly into Kingsgate, which is one of the City gates. At this point, the City walls and the Close wall become one and the houses of Cheyney Court are built into the walls.

This corner, by careful restoration, has been kept in remarkably good preservation. The little wing of the building on the right extending over the gate, is known as the Porter's Lodge. The great oak doors are much 'younger' than the gateway itself; but even these are about three hundred years old.

As late as 1859, Cheyney Court was, in fact, still some sort of law court, which it had been for centuries.

Cheyney Court, Winchester.

g. Ludlow, Northwood.

15. THE PRIOR'S GATE

My illustration shows the outside of this grand old gateway as seen from St. Swithun's Street leading into the Cathedral Close. The inside view of the gate adjoining Cheyney Court is equally fine.

It was built originally as the main gate into this part of the Close. It is not one of the City gates but stands within a few yards of the King's Gate where the city walls and those of the monastery become one. As one gate without the other would have been of little use, it is probable that they are of the same period and have stood here for five hundred years or more. The fine iron-studded oak doors are comparatively new and were probably made in the 17th century. The Royal Coat of Arms which surmount the gateway add dignity and colour to this aspect of Prior's Gate.

In the top right hand corner of the illustration one can see another view of the Porter's Lodge.

As you stand facing the Prior's Gate and turn to your right, you will see the inside of the King's Gate. The stairway on its right leads into the tiny Church of St. Swithun, which is actually built over the gate.

Creeping over the Porter's Lodge and through the embattlements of the gateway, are the trailing tendrils of the very old and beautiful wistaria which adorns the Inner Gate and Cheyney Court.

It may be worth remembering that the Prior's Gate closes at 10 p.m.

THE PRIORS' GATE, WINCHESTER.

16. THE KINGSGATE

" Sculptured bold in ponderous stone."

ANON.

Winchester once had at least six gates—one for each point of the compass and the Kingsgate and the small Durngate to the north-east, but of these only two remain, the Westgate and the Kingsgate. With Wykeham's College, really St. Mary's College, and the growing district of Kingsgate Street outside the City, the Kingsgate must always have been a great convenience. The first mention of a gate on this site was made in the twelfth century Winchester Survey but most of the existing building appears to belong to the fourteenth century. It is massively built of stone, supported to some extent by timber pillars, which separate the narrow roadway from the footpaths on either side.

Above the gate is the tiny church of St. Swithun-upon-Kingsgate, the first record of which is in the thirteenth century. Churches over city gates were not uncommon in the Middle Ages, but today such gates are few and churches over them even fewer, which makes St. Swithun's of remarkable interest, although there is little to see inside the church. The approach to it is by way of an enclosed timbered staircase with a tiny bell chamber above it. This stairway and bell chamber have recently been very well restored and considerable work has been done on the gate itself.

Beside the gate, on the east, is an unusual little shop owned by the City. From the east side of the Kingsgate starts the finest stretch of the City walls remaining today. They may be followed along College Street and the Weirs Footpath almost to the City Bridge.

King's Gate · Winchester.

17. RUINS OF WOLVESEY CASTLE

" . . . From yonder ivy-mantled tower,
The moping owl doth to the moon complain."

THOMAS GRAY.

A small gateway under the limes in College Street leads into Pilgrims School playing field and thence to the ruins. Men have lived on this site for at least 2,000 years. It was a pre-Roman settlement and in Saxon times many kings and bishops lived here. On the outer walls, the bodies of Danish pirates were hung as a warning to other invaders who should come up the Itchen.

These are memories of long ago—as is the name ' Wolvesey ' which is the ' Isle of Wolves '—a reminder of the days when these animals roamed over southern England and the ancient River Itchen meandered past islands and through marshes.

The ruins of today are those of the castle built by Bishop de Blois; the illustration shows the north end of his great hall. It stood intact until it was destroyed by the puritans during the Civil War five hundred years later. After the Restoration a new palace was built by Sir Christopher Wren for Bishop Morley. In 1785 the Wren building was demolished except for the West wing, which remains the official home of the Bishop of Winchester.

The ruins shows many examples of Norman details and some traces of the earlier Saxon and Roman work. These include some herring-bone flint work in the outer walls. The visitor is bound to notice the incongruous tile work fitted into the ancient arches. This restoration work was carried out in the 1920's.

When I visited the ruins in 1966 there was considerable archaeological digging going on. This will certainly add to our knowledge of Wolvesey. I was told of two especially interesting ' finds '—some bronze chain mail in good condition and a silver coin of King Canute under whose reign (1016–1035) England was part of a Scandinavian Empire.

OLVESEY RUINS, WINCHESTER.

18. COLLEGE GATEWAY

*" Next Wykeham's art obtain their splendid place
The zeal of Inigo, the strength of Wren."*

LIONEL JOHNSON.

In the late fourteenth century William of Wykeham chose the site
for his new school near the entrance to his Palace of Wolvesey. The
great gate, built in 1393, like the buildings of the school itself, is on the
grand scale, which he also favoured in his other foundation at Oxford,
New College. Very few buildings of this date, other than churches,
exist at all for stone was not generally used at this time except for
ecclesiastical or military purposes.

William of Wykeham was probably not the architect of the building
although his knowledge of the subject was undoubted as he was at one
time ' supervisor of the King's works in Windsor ' and he left the vast
nave of Winchester Cathedral as the finest memorial of his architectural
skill.

From the outside, the College buildings on either side of the gate
cannot be regarded as beautiful. To the east is the Warden's Lodging
and to the west stretch the brewery, the slaughterhouse and the wood
house which is now a Library—a long line of blank flint walls, broken
only by small slit windows. New College, Oxford, shows a similar
feature because, no doubt, it was wise in those days to make entry
difficult.

It is said that shortly after its erection, the great gate of Winchester
College began to subside, which accounts for the massive buttresses on
the road side.

The beauty of College, like that of the Cathedral nave, is to be found
inside.

Outer Gateway
The College, Winchester.

19. THE TRUSTY SERVANT

" A Trusty Servant's Portrait would you see,
This Emblematic Figure well survey:"

This ' strange device ' is a familiar motif to the people of Winchester.
They may have seen the large oil painting of it hanging near the stairway leading from Chamber Court of College; or, perhaps, they will
have seen it embossed on a leather drinking jack, carved on a bread-
board or engraved on silverware. In spite of its frequent occurrence
as a Winchester symbol, few would know the elaborate symbolism of
the odd accoutrements of this strange creature.

My illustration shows it as it appears on the painting in College. It
is the work of William Cave, in the year 1800. The College Coat of
Arms appears in the top left-hand corner with a rural landscape forming
the background.

The symbolism explains the qualities of this ideal servant and is
given in this doggerel painted beside the picture in College:

" A Trusty Servant's Portrait would you see,
This Emblematic Figure well survey:
The Porker's Snout, not Nice in diet shows,
The Padlock Shut, no Secrets He'll disclose:
Patient, the Ass, His Master's wrath will hear:
Swiftness in Errand, the Stagg's Feet declare:
Loaded his Left Hand apt to Labour saith:
The Vest, his Neatness: Open Hand his Faith
Girt with his Sword, his Shield upon his Arm,
Himself & Master He'll protect from harm."

THE TRUSTY SERVANT.

20. WAR MEMORIAL CLOISTERS—COLLEGE

" They went with songs to battle, they were young,
Straight of limb, true of eye, steady and aglow."

LAURENCE BINYON.

The Cloisters are a memorial to Wykehamists who lost their lives in the two World Wars. They form a ' thoroughfare ', a Via Sacra, used daily by hundreds of College men and members of the public. The Cloisters may be entered from Kingsgate Street or through the wrought iron gates from Meads.

My illustration was drawn beneath the giant plane trees and looking through these gates towards the central Cross. The atmosphere of permanent peace and dignity must surely be felt by all who pause here for a few moments.

The materials of the Cloisters—Hampshire flints, Portland stone, timber, wrought iron and heraldic tinctures, together with the smooth lawns, scarlet geraniums and rosemary bushes, make something beautiful and lasting and have a splendid unity.

The wrought iron gates and the trumpeting angels were designed by Professor Gleadowe, a former Art Master at College. They are a fine example of this ancient English craft. Above the gates on the outside is a Virgin and Child in stone which is the work of Sir Charles Wheeler. Sir Herbert Baker, the architect of this beautiful memorial, is commemorated by his monogram in gold on the roof just inside the gates. The central Cross with two sentinel Crusaders is the work of Alfred Turner, A.R.A.

A most interesting feature of the Cloisters is the continuous inscription, which starts in the north-east corner with the words ' Thanks be to God for the service of these five hundred Wykehamists ' . . . and continues on all four sides of the quadrangle. The Lombardic letters and the borders are cut from solid stone with the interstices chiselled out to a depth of several inches and filled with knapped flints.

WAR MEMORIAL CLOISTERS,
COLLEGE, WINCHESTER.

21. THE CHURCH OF ST. CROSS

" Hail! Pious roofs, by grateful Henry raised
Where toil worn age may rest, and Christ be praised."

HUMBERT.

In 1137 Henry of Blois, Bishop of Winchester and a grandson of the Conqueror, founded the Hospital of St. Cross and himself supervised much of the actual building.

This ' foundation ' provides to this day a home for " eighteen poor men," who may be recognised by their black gowns, flat hats and silver cross crosslets.

The Church and ambulatory seen in the drawing, together with Beaufort Hall and the Brothers' homes, form an open square of mellow buildings, which exclude the blustering winds from the gracious lawns and flower beds, even as they seem to exclude the bustling world from the fortunate few who live here in the evening of their lives.

Like many good things, the Church of St. Cross grew slowly and so, as we move from the east end to the nave, the north porch and the west end, we see a gradual change from the Norman style of architecture to that of the thirteenth century. In this respect, and in its cruciform plan and short square tower, the Church resembles the great Cathedral visible across the Water Meadows.

CHURCH OF SAINT CROSS, WINCHESTER.

22. BEAUFORT HALL, ST. CROSS

" The houseless wanderer
Footsore and famished, no sleek menial finds
To spurn him from that gate; the Brother there
Welcomes each outcast of the churlish world
And for his hunger carves the wheaten loaf,
And fills the goblet to his thirsting lip."

HUMBERT.

Cardinal Beaufort added the Hall to the buildings and in 1446 founded the Order of Noble Poverty, which provides for the maintenance of nine professional men who have come by hard times. They may be distinguished from the Brothers of the black robed Order of Henry of Blois by their purple robes and a silver Cardinal's badge in place of the silver cross.

Inside Beaufort Hall is the beautiful old refectory and many of its interesting and well preserved utensils. In the centre of the Hall is the open hearth and above it the louvre in the roof. The attractive stairway from the Hall led originally to the Master's Chambers in the tower and over the Porter's Lodge. The Master of St. Cross now lives in a separate house on the other side of the road.

The verse quoted above was written by the Reverend L. M. Humbert, Master of St. Cross nearly a hundred years ago, and refers to the Wayfarer's Dole. This is a gift of bread and ale, which is still given freely, now in smaller token form, to those who request it at the Porter's Lodge.

BEAUFORT HALL, SAINT CROSS, WINCHESTER.

S. Northeast del. 1950.

23. ST. CROSS FROM THE ARCHWAY

" Pass we beneath the lodge
See where, with silver cross upon his breast,
The Porter stands."

HUMBERT.

This is the archway leading into the quadrangle of St. Cross Hospital.   Through it, every year, pass thousands of visitors who come to see and hear about this remarkable ' foundation '.   They are assisted in this by the ' duty Brother '.   It is one of the regulations that each Brother in turn must act as guide to the visitors.

Beneath this arch on the left is the hatchway of the Porter's Lodge, and it is from here that he daily serves the Wayfarer's Dole.

On the left of the drawing under the old Infirmary is the opening arcading of the ambulatory—a covered promenade for the use of elderly inhabitants in bad weather.   Between the gnarled locust tree and the buttress on the transept is a well preserved late Norman window. Inside this transept, on the east side, can be seen the famous ' bird window ', which is a rare example of late Norman decoration as it is composed of birds' heads.

The long regular shadows which fall across the lawns and path are cast by the tall chimneys of the Brothers' Quarters, which form the west side of the quadrangle.

The figure in the foreground is a Brother wearing his long gown and flat hat which is a familiar sight in Winchester.

The Church of St. Cross
(12th Century) Winchester

24. IN THE CHURCH OF ST. CROSS

" With antique pillars massy proof
And storied windows richly dight,
Casting a dim, religious light."

MILTON.

A hundred years ago the interior of St. Cross Church was sadly in need of attention. The whole building was damp, the floors were broken and uneven and the seating was mixed and unsuitable. So in 1860 the Master determined to remedy these faults and today when we enter the church we are at once aware that we are in a beautiful building, beautifully kept.

We are struck immediately by its substantial dignity and fine proportions crowned by the imposing altitude of the simple vaulted ceiling. The choir and transepts are remarkably fine specimens of late transitional Norman architecture, which show rich mouldings and arcading of semi-circular interlacing arches. These are thought by some authorities to be the origin of the thirteenth century lancet windows. This part of the church is the work of Henry of Blois. The west part of the church is later work showing a gradual change of style, best seen in the aisle windows.

A small feature, which interests and delights me, is the series of ' poppy heads ' on the pew ends. Each one is decorated with a different plant, sensitively cut, and pleasant both to see and to feel. They were carved by celebrated wood-workers of the City, the Laverty brothers.

- IN THE CHURCH OF SAINT CROSS -
WINCHESTER

D 2

25. ST. CROSS FROM THE LILY POND

" And here within the surface of the river
The shadows of the massy temples lie,
And never are erased—but tremble ever."

SHELLEY.

This drawing was made from across the lily pond in the private
garden of the Master.   From this north-easterly aspect we see the pure
Norman masonry of the chancel, the tower and the north transept.
We also see, to the right of the Church, the back of the two storeyed
ambulatory, which connects the north transept by a covered way with
the main gate.   The upper storey of the building was the Infirmary,
with a window at the end for the benefit of the sick to enable them to
look into the Church.

This, I think, is the most serene and lovely view of St. Cross.   The
grey-green stones weathered for eight hundred years, the warm terra-
cotta walls of the ambulatory, the stately trees and the level lawns
together compose an unforgettable picture, all reflected in the tranquil
water of the lily pond.

Saint Cross Church
from the Lily Pond. Winchester.

26. ANCIENT HOUSES, ST. CROSS

" With weather stains upon the walls,
And stairways worn, and crazy doors,
And creaking and uneven floors,
And chimneys huge and tiled and tall,
A region of repose it seems."

ANON.

This fine block of old timber-framed houses stands on the corner of Back Street and Cripstead Lane and probably dates from the fifteenth century, which makes it contemporary with Beaufort Hall and the domestic buildings of St. Cross Hospital. Indeed it seems likely that the heavy stone used in the great chimney on the right of the cottages came from the same quarry. The gable end of the house facing us in the picture, with its generous overhang, has a heavy bargeboard and timbers held together by wooden pins. This is typical of medieval domestic architecture found in the county.

In the drawing we see ahead of us Back Street, running down to the ancient church. Although this road is only a few hundred yards from the very busy main Winchester-Southampton road, properly known as Front Street, it is a quiet domestic backwater. If we turn left by the old gas lamp post, within a few yards we cross a footbridge over a stream and are in the midst of the lush water-meadows, through which meander many fascinating little rivulets. Across the meads, and always in sight, is St. Catherine's Hill with its well known clump of beeches at the top, and the white scar of the chalk pit on its side. To an artist working in any medium, this is an area offering an endless supply of subjects all within a few delightful acres.

ANCIENT HOUSES (PRE-TUDOR), BACK STREET, SAINT CROSS, WINCHESTER.

27. THE CITY MILL

" ... *from the bridge I lean'd to hear*
The mill dam rushing down with noise,
And see the minnows everywhere
In crystal eddies glance and poise."

TENNYSON.

My drawing shows the south side of the mill, as seen from the City Bridge, each of which stands astride the River Itchen, which at Winchester is a clear bustling little stream running along to the Weirs, the walls of Wolvesey College, the water-meadows and to St. Cross.

There has been a watermill here for many hundreds of years, but up to the time of Henry VIII and the Dissolution of the Monasteries, it was owned by the Abbey of Wherwell, after which the site was given to the citizens of Winchester but the mill itself was derelict.

It was not until 1744 that the mill was rebuilt and became in fact ' the City Mill ', which ground corn for the citizens. This it continued to do until about 1900, when it ' retired ' from active life. Later it was reconditioned, given to the National Trust and let to the Youth Hostels Association and is now one of their most popular hostels. Those who visit it can have the thrilling and exhilarating experience of bathing in the mill race by hanging on a rope.

The little bridge, from which this drawing was made, is a pleasing example of small bridge building and was constructed in 1813. Engraved on a plaque is the following inscription: " The first bridge on this site was built by St. Swithun (852-863)."

THE CITY MILL, WINCHESTER, REBUILT 1744.

28. ST. JOHN'S CROFT AND THE BLUE BOAR INN

" Simple was its noble architecture.
Each ornament arrested, as it were,
in its position seemed to have
been placed there of necessity."

VOLTAIRE.

The drawing facing this page was made from a small public green off St. Giles' Hill in an elevated position to the north east of the City.

St. John's Croft is a dignified and attractive group of buildings, probably dating in its present state from the early 18th century.   The main block is hung with false bricks which conceal stone and timber work, a disguise used at that time to make old country houses resemble the fashionable red brick London houses of that day.   The porchway makes a pleasing focal point on the house and is typical of this period of domestic architecture, which is well represented in Winchester.

The entire history of this block of buildings is confused and un-certain.   Documental references go back several hundred years earlier to a row of five tenements, some of which belonged to Winchester College, during the 15th century.

St. John's Croft has been known in the past as 36 St. John's Hill and St. John's House and the district was called in early days " Bubbes' Place set in the Soke of Winton", according to Winchester College documents.

The Blue Boar Inn, sometimes called the Blue Ball Inn, is certainly one of the very oldest domestic buildings in Winchester.   It has survived from the 14th century until 1966, when the gib of a passing crane destroyed the upper storey.   This unfortunate accident occurred just at a time when the dilapidated building was about to be restored. I am glad to hear that, in spite of this setback, the restoration is still to be carried out.

ST. JOHN'S CROFT AND THE BLUE BOAR INN, WINCHESTER.

J.Northeast 1966.

29. CHESIL RECTORY

" No calculations of stresses or strains,
And not a thought for pipes or drains,
Vexed the mind of the craftsman when
He builded this house on the river strand,
With instinct sure and skilful hand."

ANON.

The word ' chesil ' means a beach and in this connection one recalls the Chesil Bank on the Dorset coast. Originally when the River Itchen was much wider than it is now, there was a beach at this spot.

Little is known of the history of this house but it is undoubtedly four to five hundred years old, when probably most houses in Winchester were similar in structure. Time, beetles and fire have accounted for the majority of them. Some think that during the Reformation the house became the Rectory of St. Peter's, Chesil—hence its name today. By the end of the nineteenth century it fell into disrepair and was condemned by the City authorities as unfit for human habitation. It was saved, however, by a firm of wood-carvers, who restored it carefully as a medieval house, for use as a furniture showroom.

Before restoration the front was entirely covered with plaster, marked to look like blocks of stone, and the beams inside were also covered with plaster. It was the fashion during the nineteenth century to make old buildings look like new ones. When the wood-carvers removed the plaster, inside and out, the beautiful timber frame was exposed. It is interesting architecturally, as it shows the method of construction. It was first completely framed together with massive oak beams, and then the interstices were filled with brick on the ground floor and lath and plaster above.

It is good to see that this ancient house has been completely and carefully restored by an enlightened City authority.

The Oldest House in Winchester, Chesil Rectory, 15th century.   J.R. Northeast 1950.

30. ST. JOHN'S HOSPITAL

" Just as old age is creeping on apace,
And clouds come over the sunset of our day,
They kindly leave, though not alone
But in good company."

BYRON.

The Hospital of St. John the Baptist, situated on both sides of the Broadway, is near King Alfred's Statue. On the north side of the High Street is St. John's House, the Chapel and some alms-houses, whilst on the south side are more alms-houses and a very pleasant garden courtyard. The original foundation was by St. Brinstan, the Bishop of Winton, in the tenth century, making it one of the oldest charities in the country. The foundation was revived by the generosity of John Devenish in 1289. Its purpose was stated as "for sick and lame soldiers, poor pilgrims and necessitated wayfaring men, to have their lodging and diet gratis for one night or longer as their inability to travel may require." At various times during its long history, numerous gifts of land and property have been made by philanthropic persons to it. In common with other charities it suffered by having most of its property and possessions confiscated during the Reformation. Cromwell was, however, constrained to leave the bare building to the Mayor and Bailiffs of the City and much of the property was later restored.

The Chapel of St. John the Baptist was founded and endowed possibly by Richard Devenish, and portions of the ancient refectory can be traced under the present hall. Here the election of the Mayors and the business of the City used to be conducted. At the rear of the Chapel is a 14th century stone head of Christ with a nimbus and cross built into a wall.

The present buildings on the south side, which are illustrated in my drawing, were designed by the architect William Garbett and built in 1833. A memorial in the Cathedral commemorates this fact. The alms-houses on the north of the High Street were erected in 1852.

At present there are forty-four inmates, and when I visited the Hospital recently, I was shown a register of their names dating back to 1835.

—THE COURTYARD, SAINT JOHN'S HOSPITAL, WINCHESTER.—

31. ABBEY HOUSE

" This false façade of towers and crenellations,
No fortress hides ".

ANON.

Abbey House was built in 1751 for the Recorder of Winchester, on part of the site of St. Mary's Abbey, from which it gets its name.

It is now the official residence of the Mayor of Winchester, as is indicated by the City Arms on the iron gates. Many visitors pause for a moment to watch the trout suspended in the clear little stream passing under the footpath. This water is one of the many branches of the River Itchen and in the last century it was still to be seen in the roadway of Middle Brook Street. Unfortunately, its course now is mainly underground.

The front of the Abbey House is pleasant enough, in a somewhat false nineteenth century way, for it is obviously a mere façade hiding a a plainer eighteenth century building. The modest but genuine beauty of Abbey House is its mellow south side, overlooking the Abbey Gardens. These, although limited, are more attractive than most small public gardens. This is largely due to the water which flows on two sides. The Doric style portico, which stands on a little bridge over one of these streams, is a pleasant relic of old-fashioned garden architecture.

The Abbey House, Winchester.

32. KING ALFRED'S STATUE

" Behold a pupil of the monkish gown,
The pious Alfred, King to justice dear!
Lord of the harp and liberating spear."

WORDSWORTH.

Hamo Thornycroft's fine statue of King Alfred was unveiled in 1901, a thousand years after the death of the monarch. It stands in splendid dignity at the bottom of the Broadway and must be remembered by all who have visited Winchester.

The bronze figure, some eighteen feet high, stands on two huge granite monoliths, so that the Saxon King looks down on the city traffic and even on to the tops of the tall buses crawling at his feet.

The figure of Alfred has an easy, relaxed pose and shows us the helmet, mantle and round leather shield of the Saxons. Raised high in Alfred's right hand is the cross-hilted sword, a symbol of Christianity, which he was to spread over much of his kingdom.

The drawing shows St. Giles' Hill in the background and the alms-houses of St. John's Hospital on the right.

King Alfred, Founder of the Kingdom and Education
—died 901 a.d. Statue erected at Winchester 1901 a.d. —